THE TALENTED T

HISTORICAL AND PRESENT: WRITERS

VOLUME 1

OCTAVIA BUTLER

PHILLIS WHEATLEY

ALICE WALKER

RICHARD WRIGHT

RALPH ELLISON

LANGSTON HUGHES

JAMES BALDWIN

LORRAINE HANSBERRY

ZORA NEALE HURSTON

MAYA ANGELOU

RITTEN BY:
SHLEY FEAZELL

LUSTRATED BY:
L-TARIQ HARRIS

THE TALENTED TENTH

HISTORICAL AND PRESENT: WRITERS

VOLUME 1

OCTAVIA BUTLER

RALPH ELLISON

PHILLIS WHEATLEY

ALICE WALKER

RICHARD W

LANGSTON HUGHES

JAMES BALDWIN

LORRAINE HANSBERRY

ZORA NEALE HURSTON

MAYA ANGELOU

10
TALENTEDTENTH
PUBLICATIONS

WRITTEN BY:
ASHLEY FEAZELL

ILLUSTRATED BY:
AL-TARIQ HARRIS

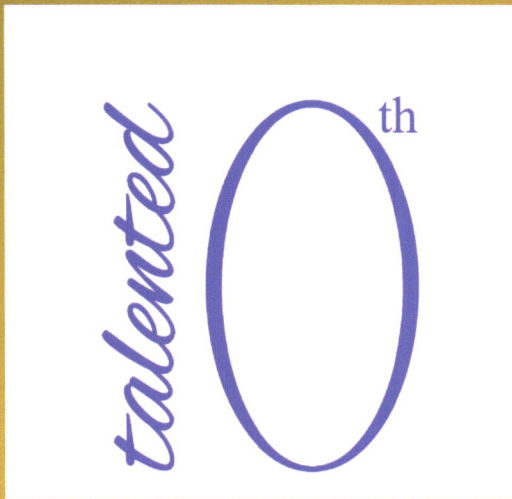

www.thetalented10th.net

Paperback edition 2020

For more information about special discounts for bulk purchases, please contact ashley@thetalented10th.net or call 323-395-3787

ISBN   978-0-9994620-8-9

INDEX

Introduction

Everyone is special. We all have certain things we can do better than others. This is our talent, and it is our responsibility to acknowledge it, and use it for good. In the Talented Tenth: Historical and Present, we will acknowledge and highlight the achievements', and talents of our culture's historical and present figures. These books will explore the vast Pan-African community and focus on its greatness. Each book will focus on 10 specific figures.

In this book The Talented Tenth: Historical and Present, one will discover authors, writers, journalist, poets, play-writes and novelist. These 10 figures have been instrumental in depicting the culture and telling the stories of Pan Africans to the world.

Alice Walker

1944-

Alice Malsenior Walker was born February 9, 1944 in Eatonton, Georgia. She was born the eighth child to two black sharecroppers and her mother also did seamstress work to help with family expenses. Walker became enthralled with reading and writing after she was accidentally shot in the eye with a BB gun. The incident made Walker very shy and self-conscious. She went to Butler Baker high school the only high school available for black people in her town at the time, and graduated valedictorian.

Walker attended Spelman College, on a scholarship and was mentored by Howard Zinn. She studied abroad in East Africa while at Sarah Lawrence and graduated with a degree in 1965. Walker is also famous for her activism, meeting Dr. Martin Luther King Jr when she was a senior in college, the meeting helped her decision to return to the south. She even took part in the 1965 "March on Washington". Her first book of poems "Once", were published in 1969 and she is famous for her work "The Color Purple", for which she earned a Pulitzer Prize. The book was turned into a movie directed by Steven Spielberg. Walker's writing often examined the treatment of African Americans, giving an observant account of everyday life.

Alice Walker is a social worker, activist, teacher and famous writer, writing about the struggles of African Americans, creating a mirror for society to see those that are not clearly visible.

Octavia Butler

1947-2006

Octavia Butler was born June 22, 1947, in Pasadena, California. She was born to two black parents, her mother a maid, and her father a shoe-shine man. Shortly after her birth her father died, and her mother raised her as a single parent. She was a quiet child and did not start writing until her teens.

Butler's small recognition allowed her to attend the Clarion workshops which focused on science-fiction. She attended University of California Los Angeles where she perfected her writing. Her writing often examined the social injustices of black people and women, ideas not popular with readers in Butler's early career. She worked several jobs to take care of herself financially and wrote novels early in the morning before work. One of her most famous trilogies includes "Kindred", "Wild Seed", and "Clay's Ark". She has won several Hugo Awards, and the first science fiction writer to win the John D & Catherine T MacArthur fellowship award. The award-winning novels "Bloodchild" and "Parable of Talents" are both set in the future. The stories written by Butler explored social conflicts through the lens of a strong protagonist. Her book settings range from past to distant future.

Butler is the first African American to win the Nebula award for science fiction writers. She was inducted into the Science Fiction Hall of Fame in 2010. Octavia Butler takes social norms and meshes them with scientific imagery to paint a vivid world of possibilities.

Langston Hughes

1902-1967

Langston Hughes was born James Mercer Langston Hughes February 1, 1902, in Joplin Missouri. It is believed that both of his paternal grandfathers were the slave masters of the plantations his grandmothers resided. His mother and father separated shortly after his birth and Hughes was primarily raised by his maternal grandmother. After the death of his grandmother, he settled with is mother in Ohio.

Hughes began writing as a teen, and after high school he was accepted into Columbia University but dropped out. Working on a steam ship he was able to travel spending time in France, West Africa, and Mexico. Traveling helped Hughes broaden his views on the social injustices African Americans endure. He was hired to work for W.E.B Dubois which proved to be beneficial , as Dubois edited some of Hughes first poems, and he worked for Carter G Woodson which allowed him to meet poet Vachel Lindsay. He eventually finished his college studies at Lincoln University with fellow alumni Thurgood Marshall, Cab Calloway, and Kwame Nkrumah. Spending time between Harlem and Pennsylvania until he committed to Harlem being his home. The unofficial "Mayor of Harlem" he welcomed all new coming artist to the city during the Harlem Renaissance. Hughes wrote plays, novels, and short stories, and formed a literary group called "Fire" which included Zora Neale Hurston John P. Davis, Bruce Nugent, Aaron Douglas, Eric Walrond, Helene Johnson, Dorothy West, and other writers of the time . He is said to be the first African American to support themselves solely on income gained from writing.

Hughes is credited with being one of the leaders of the Harlem Renaissance, an innovator in the art of jazz writing. Langston Hughes an African American writer with a great sense of racial pride.

Phillis Wheatley

1753-1784

Phillis Wheatley was born in 1753 in Senegal/Gambia West Africa. It is unknown exactly where she was taken from, or her true name. She was captured and sold into American slavery and bought by the Wheatley family. A ship named the "Phillis" brought Wheatley to Boston where she was tutored and taught to read by her owner's wife, daughter, and son, she was given the name of the ship she traveled on. By age 12 she could read Greek and Latin text.

Wheatley published her first poem in 1767 at age 14. She and her owner's son, John left America, for London to find patronage in hopes of getting her book of poems published. Wheatley found patronage from an English countess and in 1773 Phillis published her book of poems, making her the first slave and African American to publish a book of poems, and the third woman. To prove she had written the book, 17 Boston men tested to the book's authenticity including John Hancock. She continued to write and gain public recognition and was invited to dine with General George Washington to which she accepted. Once Wheatley received emancipation finding a publisher to publish her work proved impossible. Many of the Wheatly's died and with the Revolutionary War looming over the colonies her writing began losing public intrigue.

Wheatley is known for being the first African American to publish a book of poetry in the colonies but political unrest and social upheaval, stifled her career. She only published one book and had to work menial jobs to survive.

Richard Wright

1908-1960

Richard Wright was born Richard Nathaniel Wright September 4, 1908, on a plantation in Roxie, Mississippi near Natchez. Both of his grandfathers fought for freedom in the civil war and both parents were born free. He had a rough childhood due to his father leaving the home and his mother suffering a stroke. He was unable to go to school regularly because he had to work to help take care of the family.

Despite not attending school regularly and only receiving an 8th grade education he was able to publish his first short story at the age of sixteen. He became the Harlem editor of the "Daily Worker". Unfortunately, his communication with the communist party halted many social, and financial gain, and he fell into poverty during the great depression. In 1938 Wright wrote "Uncle Tom's Children" an acclaimed collection of short stories, which earned him $500 and the Guggenheim Fellowship. He then wrote "Native Son" in 1940 which catapulted him into stardom and financial freedom, it's the first book written by an African American to be selected for the Book of the Month Club. "Black Boy" came next which explored Wright's childhood and southern upbringing plagued with poverty. Both gave him notoriety and examine the unfair treatment of African Americans during the early 20th century. Wright never bonded with American society or totally agreed with communism he withdrew from society and moved to France.

An American author Richard Wright is a misunderstood wordsmith that never hesitated to expose the camouflaged areas of American black living.

Zora Neale Hurston

1891-1960

Zora Neale Hurston was born January 7, 1891, in Notasulga, Alabama, but her family quickly moved to Eatonville, Florida. She was the fifth of eight children, and both maternal and paternal grandparents were slaves. Her father was a preacher and carpenter, and her mother was a schoolteacher. When she was young her family moved to one of the first all black towns in America. When she wrote she would often use this town as the setting for her stories.

She attended Morgan Academy, a high school apart of Morgan State college but became a maid for a theatrical company to help pay for living expenses. She also worked as a manicurist, a nightclub waitress, and in a barbershop. In and out of school due to financial hardship, she persisted and finished public high school by removing ten years from her date of birth. She went on to attend Howard University and became one of the first members of sorority Zeta Phi Beta. She won a scholarship to Barnard College to study anthropology under Franz Boas. She earned a degree in anthropology and continued studies a while at Columbia University. Hurston famously wrote about the African experiences in the world, also a black woman's experience. She published many short stories and essays in the magazine "Opportunity". One of the established writers of the Harlem Renaissance, she was revered amongst her peers and a founder of "Fire" with Langston Hughes. She earned a Guggenheim award and travelled to Haiti studying voodoo and wrote "Their Eyes were Watching God", considered her masterpiece. The book was formatted for television in 2005, and her biography about Cujo Lewis "Barracoon: The Story of the Last Black Cargo", was published after her death.

A poet, novelist, and journalist Zora Neale Hurston's passion willed society to understand the black people of the world and produced timeless work.

Ralph Ellison

1914-1994

Ralph Waldo Ellison was born Oklahoma City, Oklahoma, to Lewis Alfred Ellison and Ida Millsap, on March 1, 1914. Named after Ralph Waldo Emerson, his father hoped he would grow to be a poet. After his father's death the family moved north for a while but moved back south once times got hard. Ellison worked several jobs as a teen to help the family financially. He became interested in music and played the trumpet.

Accepted into Tuskegee College as a trumpet player, Ellison's college career wasn't pleasant, often feeling like an outsider, this is when he began writing. He left Tuskegee just short of completing a bachelor degree and moved to New York. Although Ellison intended to return to Tuskegee the Great Depression hualted his return south. He met Langston Hughes, who introduced him to Richard Wright and Alain Locke. Ellison worked as editing manager of the "The Negro Quarterly", while writing reviews for Wright and the Communist party. He joined the marines during World War II and was a cook. After the war he began writing "Invisible Man". This novel was ranked nineteenth of one-hundred English novels of the 20th century by the Modern Library and won the National Book Award in 1953. "Invisible Man" remained on the Best Sellers list for sixteen weeks.

Ellison was never able to complete a second novel while alive, but his first is said to be a masterpiece. "Juneteenth", Ellison's second novel was published in 1999 after his death. A literary genius Ralph Ellison's relevance in the literary world became solidified with one novel.

Maya Angelou

1928-2014

Maya Angelou was born Marguerite Ann Johnson April 4, 1928, in St. Louis, Missouri. She was born to two black parents, that divorced before she turned four. Angelou and her older brother were sent to live with their grandmother in Stamps, Arkansas. They were moved back to their mothers and shortly after Maya was raped by her mother's boyfriend. She was sent back to live with her grandmother again. She spoke the name of her abuser, and he died shortly after. Angelou thought her abuser's death was caused by her disclosure and became mute. She didn't speak and read books all day given to her by a family friend.

When she moved to Oakland, California with her mother, she also attended California Labor School to study dance and acting, she also became the first black cable car conductor. She married Tosh Angelos and had her first kid at 17, a son. The marriage was short, and during this time Angelou began stage performing the Calypso. Times were hard and Angelou had to perform menial jobs to survive as a single mother. She started touring with Alvin Ailey as "Al & Rita" and performed on and off Broadway. James Baldwin helped Angelou become a member of the Harlem Writers Guild and she wrote musical revues to support SCLC in the civil rights movement. She helped both civil rights leaders Martin Luther King Jr, and Malcolm X organize before their assassinations. Angelou has been nominated for both Tony and Emmy awards for play "Look Away" and miniseries "Roots". During her travels abroad she began learning the languages of the countries she toured. She held teaching positions at many universities including Wake Forest and University of Ghana, without ever earning a Bachelor's degree. Some of Angelou's most famous works have been considered autobiographies. Her book "I know why the Caged bird sings" was turned into a made for tv film. Her poem collection, "Just Give me a Drink of Water Fo I Die", was nominated for a Pulitzer Prize and her poems were famously used for John Singleton's movie "Poetic Justice", Angelou even made an appearance in the film. She is the first African American woman member of the Directors Guild of America writing "Georgia Georgia" in 1972 and directing "Down in the Delta" in 1998.

Maya Angelou has received over 50 honorary degrees and has written over 30 books and awarded 3 Grammys. She is the first African American to recite a poem at a Presidential Inauguration and the second since Robert Frost. Awarded the Presidential Medal of Freedom in 2011. Through much let down and turmoil Maya Angelou was able to rise and live an extraordinary life of intellect and entertainment.

James Baldwin

1924-1987

James Arthur Baldwin was born in New York August 2, 1924. Born to two black parents his mother left his father before he was born due to abuse. His mother remarried a preacher and had 8 other kids. Baldwin was treated harsh by his step-father, which caused him to spend much time alone. He was deemed gifted at an early age.

Baldwin wrote his first article "Harlem: Then and Now" when he was thirteen and became a preacher while still in high school. After graduation and a series of odd low paying jobs Baldwin secured a literary apprenticeship in Greenwich Village with the help of Richard Wright. Self-taught he infamously wrote a series of short essays called "Native Son", and a novel "Giovanni's Room", both books had characters combating internal uncertainty while facing social intolerance. His novel "Go Tell it on the Mountain" is said to be some of his finest work. Baldwin not just a writer but also an activist, writing "Nobody Knows my Name", a book of essays exploring the dynamics of black and white people in the United States. In 1964, his paly "Blues for Mister Charlie" debuted on Broadway. The best-selling book "The Fire Next Time", was an article written in the 1967 New Yorker magazine about the Black Muslim separatist group, apart of the civil rights movement. Baldwin traveled back and forth, living between Paris and New York, and continued to write until his death publishing "If Beale Street could Talk" in 1974. His books dealt with issues concerning religion, poverty, discrimination and homophobia.

Although Baldwin was self-taught, he became a teacher at the University of Massachusetts Amherst and Hampshire College, later in life. James Baldwin was an essayist, professor, journalist and prolific writer using intricate themes to challenge the mindset of his readers.

Lorraine Hansberry

1930-1965

Lorraine Hansberry was born May 19, 1930 the youngest of four children. Her father was a successful real-estate broker, and her mother a school bus driver. Hansberry was born and raised in the Chicago area, and due to her family's wealth experienced heavy racism. When her father moved them into a neighborhood considered "white", the family was harassed, and had to take their case all the way to the Supreme Court. The Hansberry's household was greatly involved in the progression of black people. Her house was always visited by black intellectuals.

She attended University of Wisconsin-Madison for college, and studied abroad in Mexico, until she left college and moved to Harlem to pursue her writing, in 1951. She worked with Paul Robeson on the newspaper "Freedom", and married a Jewish publisher, writer, and political activist, Robert Nemiroff in 1953. The couple divorced and kept a business relationship. Hansberry was actively involved in the civil rights movement, covering injustices happening all over the world. She even met with Attorney General Robert Kennedy to discuss racial inequalities. Hansberry wrote under her initials for "The Ladder", a feminist magazine that opposed homophobia. Her most famous work, a play "A Raisin in the Sun", was acted out on Broadway, making her the first African American female author to have a play debut on Broadway. The play was named after a line in a Langston Hughes poem, "Harlem". At age 29 she was the youngest American to win a New York Critic's Circle Award. The play was turned into a film in 1961 starring Sidney Poitier. Hansberry died in 1965 of pancreatic cancer. After her death, Hansberry's ex-husband debuted a collection of her interviews and writings in an Off-Broadway adaption called "To Be Young Gifted & Black".

Hansberry's short-lived life impacted the masses. Her dedication to truth-telling found her writing amongst leading feminist and civil rights activist. Although Lorraine Hansberry did not live a long life, her writing and ideas shape the world today.

Where was Lorraine Hansberry born?

a. New York

b. Los Angeles

c. Chicago

What is Maya Angelou's birth name?

a. Mary Ann Fisher

b. Marguerite Ann Johnson

c. Marian Lorraine Kurt

Ralph Ellison was introduced to whom by Langston Hughes?

a. Richard Wright

b. Nelson Mandela

c. Maya Angelou

Octavia Butler won what science-fiction award?

a. Nebula Award

b. Cosmic Award

c. Atom Award

Which Alice Walker novel was made into a movie?

a. The Color Purple

b. Their Eyes were Watching God

c. Uncle Tom's Cabin

Zora Neale Hurston moved to what town shortly after birth?

a. Eatonville, Florida

b. Macon, Georgia

c. Selma, Alabama

Richard Wright was apart of which social/political group?

a. Socialist

b. Communist

c. Marxist

Langston Hughes was born?

a. Langston James Hughes

b. Langford Winston Hughes

c. James Mercer Langston Hughes

James Baldwin was born in what year?

a. 1908

b. 1924

c. 1948

Phillis Wheatley was born where?

a. West Africa

b. East Africa

c. South Africa

GLOSSARY

Abroad: in or to a foreign country or countries.

Activism: the policy or action of using vigorous campaigning to bring about political or social change

Broadway: Broadway theatre, also known simply as Broadway, refers to the theatrical performances presented in the 41 professional theatres, each with 500 or more seats, located in the Theater District and Lincoln Center along Broadway, in Midtown Manhattan, New York City

Calypso: a kind of West Indian (originally Trinidadian) music in syncopated African rhythm, typically with words improvised on a topical theme

Clarion workshop: Established in 1968, the Clarion Science Fiction and Fantasy Writers' Workshop is the oldest workshop of its kind and is widely recognized as a premier proving and training ground for aspiring writers of fantasy and science fiction

Communism: a political theory derived from Karl Marx, advocating class war and leading to a society in which all property is publicly owned and each person works and is paid according to their abilities and needs

Communist: a person who supports or believes in the principles of communism

Extraordinary: very unusual or remarkable

Harlem Renaissance: The Harlem Renaissance was an intellectual, social, and artistic explosion centered in Harlem, Manhattan, New York City, spanning the 1920s

Heritage: property that is or may be inherited; an inheritance

Guggenheim Fellowships: grants that have been awarded annually since 1925 by the John Simon Guggenheim Memorial Foundation to those "who have demonstrated exceptional capacity for productive scholarship or exceptional creative ability in the arts

Intellect: an intelligent or intellectual person

Intellectual: possessing a highly developed intellect

Intricate: very complicated or detailed

LGBTQ: LGBT (also acronymed as **LGBTQ** or GLBT) is an initialism that stands for lesbian, gay, bisexual, and transgender

Maternal: related through the mother's side of the family

Nebula award: The Nebula Awards annually recognize the best works of science fiction or fantasy published in the United States. The awards are organized and awarded by the Science Fiction and Fantasy Writers of America, a nonprofit association of professional science fiction and fantasy writers

Paternal: related through the father

Plantation: an estate on which crops such as coffee, sugar, and tobacco are cultivated by resident labor

Publish: print (something) in a book or journal so as to make it generally known

Racism: prejudice, discrimination, or antagonism directed against someone of a different race based on the belief that one's own race is superior

Science fiction: fiction based on imagined future scientific or technological advances and major social or environmental changes, frequently portraying space or time travel and life on other planets

Biography.com
History.com
Blackhistoryheroes.com
Black In America by Henry Louis Gates
Britannica.com
Blackpast.org
Ushistory.org
Africanknowledge.com
www.gf.org
Poetryfoundation.org
Pbs.org

www.ingramcontent.com/pod-product-compliance
Lightning Source LLC
Chambersburg PA
CBHW061152030426
42336CB00002B/25